Plan your OWN Funeral Like A PRO

Planner and Keepsake

T. Keller

ISBN: 979-8-218-07357-2

In Memory of My Loving & Beautiful Mother,

You went through and overcame so much in your life.
I'm sorry that I took the limited time we shared for granted.
You were my rock. Whenever I needed you the most you were always there.
My daughter, your granddaughter, was your best friend and we miss you so much.
You're forever in my heart. I love you for forever and a century.

Thanks for being My Mother,
-Your Oldest

In Memory of my Superhero, My Father,

It's so difficult to accept that you're gone. You've always been so strong and resilient. You never complained once during your short battle with Lung Cancer. I witnessed your efforts to live your life to the fullest despite this disease. If only we had more time. You're forever in my heart. I love you for forever and a century.

Thanks for being My Father,
-Your Oldest

TABLE OF CONTENTS

A Letter from the Founder	
Why I Love You	
All About You	1
Important	5
Family Medical History	9
Identifying Marks	13
Background	17
Funeral Arrangement	25
Obituary	29
Program Preferences	33
Memories	39
Final Letter to Loved Ones	57
Will Talk	101
Apologies	105
Growth	109
Confessions	113
Expressions	117
Pictures	121
Family Tree	141

A Letter from the Founder,

My name is Tenesia Keller, and I am the author of this self-help book.

Thank you for supporting my small business and deciding to take the next step to plan your own funeral. This book has been a passion of mine for the last five years. The idea of this booklet came to me after losing my beloved Mother.

My Mother and I did not have the best relationship when I was younger, but things changed after I became an adult. We had only just begun to strengthen that relationship, when her Type 1 diabetes took a turn for the worse, and ultimately took her life. My Mom raised me, I saw her every single day and yet our conversations were minimal. It dawned on me after her passing that there was a lot that we never discussed, a ton of questions I never got the chance to ask and a lot of emotions I never got the opportunity to express.

It's my hope and desire that this self-help job will change that for you. Some conversations are more difficult to have than others; I honestly believe that. This booklet can act as that bridge in order to fill whatever gap there is, meaning whatever conversation you are struggling to have with your loved ones. Or whichever conversation you're unable to have with your loved one, maybe they're too young to have the difficult conversations with, maybe they moved away and you feel the conversation deserves more than just a phone call, maybe there are secrets you planned to take to your grave that are beneficial/important to your loved ones, or maybe you didn't get the opportunity to say I Love You enough. Here is your opportunity to accomplish all of those things plus more.

In the 5 years that it took to work up the courage to publish this book, my Father passed away from Lung Cancer. His death was so totally unexpected. He was one of the strongest men I knew. I was sure that he could overcome anything. In February 2019, we found out he had stage 3 lung cancer. Although he stopped smoking and remained positive throughout treatment because of his desire to live, he departed from this Earth in May 2019.

Life is short. Please don't hesitate any longer. Complete your Self-help booklet today. Thank you for your support and courage to tackle this difficult challenge of planning your own funeral.

Thank you,

T. Keller

WHY I LOVE YOU!!

You purchased this book for someone you love. Tell them why you care to have this keepsake of him/her.

_____

_____

_____

_____

_____

_____

_____

_____

_____

_____

_____

_____

_____

_____

_____

_____

_____

_____

_____

_____

_____

_____

_____

_____

_____

_____

_____

ALL ABOUT YOU

ALL ABOUT YOU

Name: _____

Address: _____

_____

Sex: _____ Race: _____

Birthday: _____ SSN: _____

Spouse: _____

CIRCLE ONE: **Would you like to Donate your Organs**: YES   NO
Autopsy: YES   NO   **Donate Body to Science:** YES   NO
Other: _____

List All Medical Conditions:

_____
_____
_____
_____
_____
_____

List All Medications:

_____
_____
_____
_____
_____
_____
_____
_____
_____

Power of Attorney(s): include copy of document_____

_____

Emergency Contact Information

Name: _____

Address: _____

Number(s): _____ Relation: _____

Name: _____

Address: _____

Number(s): _____ Relation: _____

Doctors' Names, Numbers & Specialties:

_____

_____

_____

_____

_____

_____

Name of All Children (Alive and Deceased. Ordered Oldest to Youngest.)

_____

_____

_____

_____

_____

Name of God Children: _____

_____

_____

Name the Godparents of your children: _____

_____

_____

IMPORTANT

IMPORTANT

CIRCLE ONE: Are you a **Veteran**:   YES   NO

This is important because it could reduce funeral costs tremendously.

Who did you serve for? What years? Where? What was your rank? Please list name used, if changed.

_____

_____

_____

_____

_____

_____

_____

_____

_____

Do you have a **BURIAL PLOT**:   YES   NO

List Name of Church/Cemetery, Address, Person of Contact & Phone Number

_____

_____

_____

_____

_____

_____

_____

Do you have a **LIFE INSURANCE POLICY**:   YES   NO

If so, List the Name of your Insurance Company, Agent, Phone Number & Extension

_____

_____

_____

_____

_____

Do you have a **LIVING WILL**:   YES   NO

Where do you keep this, in the event of your untimely passing?

_____

_____

_____

Do you have a **WILL**:   YES   NO

If so, List Lawyers' Information here (Name, Address & Number)

_____

_____

_____

_____

_____

_____

_____

Church Home: _____

_____

_____

_____

_____

Pastor(s): _____

Church Address: _____

_____

_____

_____

_____

Church Number(s): _____

_____

Do you have ALL of your important documents in a safe place?

Important documents include but are not limited to your Will, your birth certificates, social security card, insurance documents, health insurance cards, copy of photo ID, passports, etc. Your children's birth certificates, social security card, insurance documents, health insurance cards, copy of photo ID, passports, etc.

FAMILY MEDICAL HISTORY

PLEASE LIST ALL FAMILY MEDICAL HISTORY *including any fertility issues.*

Maternal:

_____

_____

_____

_____

_____

_____

_____

_____

_____

_____

_____

_____

_____

_____

_____

_____

_____

_____

_____

_____

_____

_____

_____

_____

_____

_____

_____

Paternal:

_____

_____

_____

_____

_____

_____

_____

_____

_____

_____

_____

_____

_____

_____

_____

_____

_____

_____

_____

_____

_____

_____

_____

_____

_____

_____

_____

_____

IDENTIFYING MARKS

Identifying Marks

Please list the location of your birthmark and describe its appearance:

_____

_____

_____

_____

Please list a description of All Tattoos and Locations:

_____

_____

_____

_____

_____

Please list any visible scars that may be seen by the public and locations

_____

_____

_____

_____

Other Identifying Marks you'd like to mention:

_____

_____

_____

_____

_____

_____

_____

_____

_____

This section is for you to add pictures of those identifying marks if you like.

BACKGROUND

Background Information

Where were you born? (Please include hospital, city, state & country)

_____

_____

_____

What grade schools did you attend?

_____

_____

_____

_____

List any extracurricular activities you participated in? (sports, band, beta, etc.)

_____

_____

_____

_____

Did you graduate?   YES   NO
From where and what year? If you didn't graduate, Why not?

_____

_____

_____

_____

Did you receive any Scholarships?   YES   NO

Did you attend College?   YES   NO

If yes, What College and What degrees/certificates do you have?

_____

_____

_____

_____

If you did not attend College, Why Not? _____

_____

_____

_____

_____

List any extracurricular activities you participated in? (sports, band, beta, etc.)

_____

_____

_____

_____

Which Career Path did you take and why? _____

_____

_____

_____

_____

If you had the opportunity to do it all over again, what would you change about your education and/or career choice? _____

_____

_____

_____

_____

_____

Are you working at a job that you love?   YES   NO

Did you retire doing what you loved?   YES   NO

How old were you when you were baptized? _____

Do you remember where you were baptized and who baptized you? If so, please list: _____

_____

_____

_____

_____

Describe how you felt before and after being baptized: _____

_____

_____

_____

_____

_____

_____

_____

_____

_____

_____

_____

_____

What are your parents' names? _____

_____

What are you Grandparents' names? Maternal _____

_____

_____

Paternal Grandparents_____

_____

What are your Siblings' Names: (List Oldest to Youngest; whether alive or deceased. What number are you?)

_____

_____

_____
_____
_____
_____
_____
_____
_____
_____
_____
_____
_____
_____

Have you ever Adopted Kids or Put up any Kids for Adoption? YES NO

Why or why not? Share your story _____

_____
_____
_____
_____
_____
_____
_____
_____
_____
_____
_____
_____
_____

_____

_____

_____

_____

Have you ever Fostered any children? YES   NO How many? _____

Share your story _____

_____

_____

_____

_____

_____

_____

_____

_____

_____

_____

_____

_____

_____

_____

_____

_____

_____

Do you own any pets?   YES   NO

What kind of pets are they and what are their names?

_____

_____

_____

_____

_____

_____

_____

_____

_____

Do you have any nieces and nephews?   YES   NO

Name them along with their parent (your sibling)

_____

_____

_____

_____

_____

_____

_____

_____

_____

_____

_____

_____

_____

_____

_____

_____

_____

_____

FUNERAL

ARRANGEMENT

FUNERAL ARRANGEMENTS. Funerals can be expensive if you don't know what you want. By planning your funeral ahead of time, you are allowing yourself the option to shop around for better pricing on caskets, programs, etc., put money to the side to pay for your funeral, maintain a life insurance/burial insurance policy, etc. You will not regret the decision of planning your funeral early.

What's your funeral Budget? _____

How will you pay for your funeral? _____
_____

What funeral home do you prefer? Include Name, Number & Address
_____
_____
_____
_____

Do you want to be **Cremated**?   YES   NO   **Buried**?   YES   NO

Do you want a funeral?   YES   NO

Do you want a grave side service?   YES   NO

Where would you like your funeral to take place? _____
_____

What Pastor would you like to reside at your funeral? _____
_____

What song do you want sung and by whom? _____
_____
_____

Active Pallbearers: _____
_____
_____
_____
_____
_____
_____

Honorary Pallbearers: _____

_____

_____

_____

_____

_____

Favorite Scripture: _____

_____

_____

_____

Speaker Choices: _____

_____

_____

_____

Do you want Praise Dancers?   YES   NO

If so, what song would you like them to dance to? _____

_____

_____

_____

What colors would you like to wear? _____

Please specify if you'd like a suit, dress, blouse & pants, etc.

_____

_____

_____

_____

_____

_____

_____

_____

_____

OBITUARY

OBITUARY. A typical obituary includes your full name, birthday and/or age, city/state you resided in, date deceased, the names of your parents, siblings, and/or children, your profession, age at baptism, deceased relatives, hobbies, church home information, favorite scripture, funeral information, a picture, and where donations and gifts can be dropped off. What do you want your obituary to say?

_____

_____

_____

_____

_____

_____

_____

_____

_____

_____

_____

_____

_____

_____

_____

_____

_____

_____

_____

_____

_____

_____

_____

_____

PROGRAM
PREFERENCES

PROGRAM PREFERENCES. Programs are important. Not only does it give your family and fears something to remember you by but it also showcases photos of some memorable moments, the order of the funeral, your obituary, pallbearers, thanks to pastor, family & friends and even a personal poem written by you or your favorite poem written by someone else.

Let's set up the outside of your obituary

Pallbearers:

_____   _____
_____   _____
_____   _____

Honorary Pallbearers:

_____   _____
_____   _____
_____   _____

**PERSONAL POEM,
FAVORITE POEM, OR
POEM WRITTEN BY
CHILD(REN)**

Special Thanks to ----------------------------------

--.

FUNERAL HOME INFORMATION

In Loving Memory of

PHOTO OF
YOUR CHOICE

First & Last Name

Born
##-##-####

Died
##-##-####

Pastor & Service Location Information

BACK   FRONT

Please search online to get some ideas, if needed.

Let's discuss Wording.

What would you like your program to say? In Memory of? Home Going Service for? Farewell Service for? Final Celebration for? Celebration of Life for? Homecoming Service for? What do you prefer?

_____

_____

_____

_____

_____

When listing your dates of birth and departure how do you want it worded? Sunrise/Sunset? Born/Died? mm/dd/yyyy to mm/dd/yyyy?

_____

_____

_____

What Color Scheme would you like for your program and the text?

_____

_____

_____

The inside of your program should include your obituary, pictures (optional) and order of funeral service. Please be sure to include photos of you and photos with children/spouse, etc. The goal is to have relatives reminisce about the fun times and not see you as ill or in pain.

If you do not have any photos like this, then I highly suggest that you start taking some asap or at least find one good picture that captures your soulful personality!!!!

If you have a spouse, children and or grandchildren I suggest taking a new picture at least every 6 months either by yourself or with others. It will come in handy to create a wonderful scrapbook for those that love you. We will discuss this further later on.

Distant Relatives. Your children may not have any knowledge of out of town or estranged relatives but of course in the event that you pass those relatives/friends deserve the opportunity to come and pay their respects. This section is for the name, phone number and possible address of those loved ones.

_____

_____

_____

_____

_____

_____

_____

_____

_____

_____

_____

_____

_____

_____

_____

_____

_____

_____

_____

_____

_____

_____

_____

_____

MEMORIES

All Memorable Stories includes excitement, drama, suspense, and humor. Let's began. Everything that you include below if optional. <u>I highly recommend completing these sections</u>. This section not only gives your loved ones more insight of the life you lived before them but also display events that took place when they were too young to understand or situation/incidents that you were never able to explain or talk about openly with them for fear of rejection or misunderstanding or timing.

MEMORIES.

How did you meet your spouse? _____

_____

_____

_____

_____

_____

_____

_____

_____

What advice can you give on how to maintain a healthy marriage?

_____

_____

_____

_____

_____

_____

_____

_____

_____

_____

_____

_____

_____

_____

_____

What advice can you give to your daughter(s) or granddaughter(s) to help lead them to a healthy life with minimum regrets? _____

_____

_____

_____

_____

_____

_____

_____

_____

_____

_____

_____

_____

_____

What advice can you give to your son(s) or grandson(s) to help lead them to a healthy life with minimum regrets? _____

_____

_____

_____

_____

_____

_____

_____

_____

_____

_____

_____

_____

_____

Favorite Color(s) _____

Favorite Book(s) _____

_____

_____

Favorite Movie(s)_____

_____

_____

Favorite Actor(s)/Actress(es)_____

_____

_____

Favorite Television Show(s)_____

_____

_____

Favorite Music Artist(s)_____

_____

_____

Favorite Song(s)_____

_____

_____

Favorite Hobbies_____

_____

_____

Favorite Job(s) _____

_____

_____

_____

Favorite Car(s) _____

_____

_____

Best Friends/Relatives_____

_____

_____

What was a typical day like for you as a **CHILD?**_____

_____

_____

_____

_____

_____

What was a typical day like for you as a **TEENAGER?**_____

_____

_____

_____

_____

What was a typical day like for you as a **YOUNG ADULT?**_____

_____

_____

_____

_____

_____

What was a typical day like for you as a **MATURE ADULT?**_____

_____

_____

_____

_____

_____

_____

Where have you traveled to _____

_____

_____

_____

_____

_____

What's your take on drugs/addictions? Share your experience or concerns with your children. This section is helpful because it shows your children that you are human too. Secrets like these deserve to be shared when your child(ren), friend(s), or relative(s) are in need of an intervention for possible drug or alcohol abuse, or to explain your poor behavior to your friends/loved ones that may have witnessed your episodes the years.

_____

_____

_____

_____

_____

_____

_____

_____

_____

_____

_____

_____

_____

_____

Share your Favorite Childhood Memory: _____

_____

_____

_____

_____

_____

_____

_____

_____

_____

_____

_____

_____

_____

_____

_____

Share your Worst Childhood Memory:

_____

_____

_____

_____

_____

_____

_____

_____

_____

_____

_____

_____
_____
_____
_____

Share your Favorite Adult Memory:

_____
_____
_____
_____
_____
_____
_____
_____
_____
_____
_____
_____
_____
_____

Share your Worst Adult Memory:

_____
_____
_____
_____
_____
_____
_____

_____

_____

_____

_____

_____

_____

_____

What is the Best Decision that you've ever made?

_____

_____

_____

_____

_____

_____

_____

_____

_____

_____

_____

_____

_____

_____

_____

_____

_____

_____

_____

_____

Describe your biggest Mistake/Regret

_____
_____
_____
_____
_____
_____
_____
_____
_____
_____
_____
_____
_____
_____
_____
_____
_____
_____
_____
_____
_____
_____
_____
_____
_____
_____
_____
_____

Share something that's hard to talk about like losing a parent, a child (miscarriages count), a partner, a pet, a job, everything, etc. Your personal experiences will one day be able to comfort your loved ones in ways you may never understand. Please also be sure to describe how you were feeling in that moment, how long you were down and out, your emotional rollercoaster, how things started to turn around, and why you kept going. How were you able to put the pieces of your life back together after such a tragic loss?

_____

_____

_____

_____

_____

_____

_____

_____

_____

_____

_____

_____

_____

_____

_____

_____

_____

_____

_____

_____

_____

_____

_____

Have you ever stolen anything? What was it? What consequences followed? What lesson did you learn? _____

_____

_____

_____

_____

_____

_____

_____

_____

_____

_____

_____

_____

_____

_____

_____

Did you grow up without a parent or both parent? If so, what did you do? Who raised you? How not have your parent(s) around affect you?

_____

_____

_____

_____

_____

_____

_____

_____

_____

_____

_____

_____

_____

_____

_____

_____

_____

_____

_____

_____

_____

_____

_____

What is the craziest thing you've ever done?

_____

_____

_____

_____

_____

_____

_____

_____

What's the silliest thing you've ever done?

_____

_____

_____

_____

_____

_____

_____

_____

_____

_____

_____

_____

What is the riskiest dare you've ever accepted or the riskiest thing you've ever done?

_____

_____

_____

_____

_____

_____

_____

_____

_____

_____

_____

_____

_____

_____

_____

_____

Is there a situation that you want to discuss with your child that you never had the opportunity to discuss with your parents. Please do so below

_____

_____

_____

_____

_____

_____

_____

_____

_____

_____

_____

_____

_____

_____

_____

_____

_____

_____

_____

_____

_____

_____

_____

_____

_____

_____

_____

_____

How did you feel when you became a parent for the first time? If you have more than one child, describe your reaction and fondest memory with each one.

_____

_____

_____

_____

_____

_____

_____

_____

_____

_____

_____

_____

_____

_____

_____

_____

_____

_____

_____

_____

_____

_____

_____

_____

_____

_____

_____

_____

_____

_____

_____

FINAL LETTERS

To Spouse, Children, Parents, Siblings & Friends

Final Letter to Spouse

Dear _____,

_____

_____

_____

_____

_____

_____

_____

_____

_____

_____

_____

_____

_____

_____

_____

_____

_____

_____

_____

_____

_____

_____

_____

_____

_____

Final Letter to Child or Children

Dear _____,

_____

_____

_____

_____

_____

_____

_____

_____

_____

_____

_____

_____

_____

_____

_____

_____

_____

_____

_____

_____

_____

_____

_____

_____

_____

_____

_____

_____

Final Letter to Child or Children

Dear _____,

_____

_____

_____

_____

_____

_____

_____

_____

_____

_____

_____

_____

_____

_____

_____

_____

_____

_____

_____

_____

_____

_____

_____

_____

_____

_____

_____

_____

_____

Final Letter to Child or Children

Dear _____,

_____

_____

_____

_____

_____

_____

_____

_____

_____

_____

_____

_____

_____

_____

_____

_____

_____

_____

_____

_____

_____

_____

_____

_____

_____

_____

_____

Final Letter to Child or Children

Dear _____,

_____

_____

_____

_____

_____

_____

_____

_____

_____

_____

_____

_____

_____

_____

_____

_____

_____

_____

_____

_____

_____

_____

_____

_____

_____

_____

_____

_____

Final Letter to Child or Children

Dear _____,

_____
_____
_____
_____
_____
_____
_____
_____
_____
_____
_____
_____
_____
_____
_____
_____
_____
_____
_____
_____
_____
_____
_____
_____
_____
_____
_____
_____
_____
_____
_____
_____

Final Letter to Child or Children

Dear _____,

_____

_____

_____

_____

_____

_____

_____

_____

_____

_____

_____

_____

_____

_____

_____

_____

_____

_____

_____

_____

_____

_____

_____

_____

_____

_____

_____

_____

Final Letter to Child or Children

Dear _____,

_____

_____

_____

_____

_____

_____

_____

_____

_____

_____

_____

_____

_____

_____

_____

_____

_____

_____

_____

_____

_____

_____

_____

_____

_____

_____

_____

_____

_____

Final Letter to Child or Children

Dear _____,

_____

_____

_____

_____

_____

_____

_____

_____

_____

_____

_____

_____

_____

_____

_____

_____

_____

_____

_____

_____

_____

_____

_____

_____

_____

_____

_____

_____

Final Letter to Child or Children

Dear _____,

_____

_____

_____

_____

_____

_____

_____

_____

_____

_____

_____

_____

_____

_____

_____

_____

_____

_____

_____

_____

_____

_____

_____

_____

_____

_____

_____

_____

_____

Final Letter to Child or Children

Dear _____,

_____

_____

_____

_____

_____

_____

_____

_____

_____

_____

_____

_____

_____

_____

_____

_____

_____

_____

_____

_____

_____

_____

_____

_____

_____

_____

_____

_____

Final Letter to Parent or Parents

Dear _____,

_____
_____
_____
_____
_____
_____
_____
_____
_____
_____
_____
_____
_____
_____
_____
_____
_____
_____
_____
_____
_____
_____
_____
_____
_____
_____
_____
_____
_____
_____
_____
_____
_____
_____

Final Letter to Parent or Parents

Dear _____,

_____

_____

_____

_____

_____

_____

_____

_____

_____

_____

_____

_____

_____

_____

_____

_____

_____

_____

_____

_____

_____

_____

_____

_____

_____

_____

_____

Final Letter to Sibling or Siblings

Dear _____,

_____

_____

_____

_____

_____

_____

_____

_____

_____

_____

_____

_____

_____

_____

_____

_____

_____

_____

_____

_____

_____

_____

_____

_____

_____

_____

_____

Final Letter to Sibling or Siblings

Dear _____,

_____

_____

_____

_____

_____

_____

_____

_____

_____

_____

_____

_____

_____

_____

_____

_____

_____

_____

_____

_____

_____

_____

_____

_____

_____

_____

_____

_____

Final Letter to Sibling or Siblings

Dear _____,

_____

_____

_____

_____

_____

_____

_____

_____

_____

_____

_____

_____

_____

_____

_____

_____

_____

_____

_____

_____

_____

_____

_____

_____

_____

_____

_____

_____

_____

Final Letter to Sibling or Siblings

Dear _____,

_____

_____

_____

_____

_____

_____

_____

_____

_____

_____

_____

_____

_____

_____

_____

_____

_____

_____

_____

_____

_____

_____

_____

_____

_____

_____

_____

_____

Final Letter to Friend or Friends

Dear _____,

_____

_____

_____

_____

_____

_____

_____

_____

_____

_____

_____

_____

_____

_____

_____

_____

_____

_____

_____

_____

_____

_____

_____

_____

_____

_____

Final Letter to Friend or Friends

Dear _____,

_____

_____

_____

_____

_____

_____

_____

_____

_____

_____

_____

_____

_____

_____

_____

_____

_____

_____

_____

_____

_____

_____

_____

_____

_____

_____

_____

_____

_____

_____

Final Letter to Friend or Friends

Dear _____,

_____

_____

_____

_____

_____

_____

_____

_____

_____

_____

_____

_____

_____

_____

_____

_____

_____

_____

_____

_____

_____

_____

_____

_____

_____

_____

_____

_____

Final Letter to Friend or Friends

Dear _____,

_____

_____

_____

_____

_____

_____

_____

_____

_____

_____

_____

_____

_____

_____

_____

_____

_____

_____

_____

_____

_____

_____

_____

_____

_____

_____

_____

_____

_____

_____

_____

WILL TALK

If you don't have a **Will/Living Will** get one immediately.

Wills discuss the placement of your small children and/or pets in the event that you pass away before they are old enough to care for themselves. Wills also include life insurance policies, burial plots, or savings accounts to be used for your funeral. It includes banking information, credit card information, stocks and bonds, the deed(s) to your house(s), Mobile home(s), car(s), boat(s), motorcycle(s), etc.

If you decide that you do not want a Will then be sure to assign Power of Attorney to someone that you Trust. Power of Attorney cannot be a verbal agreement between you and the chosen party, it has to be notarized by a Notary Public. A Power of Attorney has the Power to tell the doctor to resuscitate or not resuscitate. He/She also has the power to access your personal banking information to pay for your healthcare expenses, transportations, household bills, car notes, loans, credit card bills, safe deposit boxes, etc.

It's very important to have your finances in order because you do not want to leave a huge burden of debt on the ones you loved. Start saving now, if you have not already. Make a list of all the bills you pay along with the account numbers, company names, phones numbers and addresses if possible. It will also be helpful if you can include their due dates. I also recommend that you make copies of all your credit cards both front and back so when you pass your Power of Attorney will be able to call those companies and have them cancelled.

Also, be sure to list all sources of income you may have including but not limited to unemployment, employment, 401K, retirement, Social Security, Child Support, Inheritance, Residual, etc.

List Finance Companies, Utility Companies, Mortgage Companies, Loan Companies, etc. Below you can list all the companies you pay each month, along with their names, numbers, due dates and address. This will allow your loved ones to continue taking care of your business so that all of your hard work doesn't go down the drain. Be sure to include who you pay your property taxes to, the due date, the amount, and the name that it's under if different from the name on your license.

_____

_____

_____

_____

_____

_____

_____

_____

_____

_____

_____

_____

_____

_____

_____

_____

_____

_____

_____

_____

_____

_____

_____

_____

APOLOGIES

APOLOGIES

APOLOGIES

GROWTH

GROWTH. What have you overcome??

_____
_____
_____
_____
_____
_____
_____
_____
_____
_____
_____
_____
_____
_____
_____
_____
_____
_____
_____
_____
_____
_____
_____
_____
_____
_____
_____
_____
_____

CONFESSIONS

CONFESSIONS

CONFESSIONS

EXPRESSIONS

EXPRESSIONS. Get it off your chest. What do you want to say??

_____
_____
_____
_____
_____
_____
_____
_____
_____
_____
_____
_____
_____
_____
_____
_____
_____
_____
_____
_____
_____
_____
_____
_____
_____
_____
_____
_____
_____
_____
_____
_____
_____
_____
_____

EXPRESSIONS

PICTURES

Notice that the next 16 pages are BLANK. These blank pages are for you to paste your pictures from both the past and present. I would also recommend that from this day forward you include a new updated picture of yourself taken every 6 to 12 months. Be sure to include the date the picture was taken (whether you hold up a date card in the photo or write the date on the back of the photo).

You will also find a Family Tree on Page 102. Please complete for your family.

**Place
Photos
Here**

Front & Back

**Place
Photos
Here**

Front & Back

**Place
Photos
Here**

Front & Back

Place
Photos
Here

Front & Back

**Place
Photos
Here**

Front & Back

**Place
Photos
Here**

Front & Back

Place
Photos
Here

Front & Back

Place
Photos
Here

Front & Back

FAMILY TREE

Family Tree

Paternal Great Grandparents

_____ & _____

_____ & _____

Paternal Grandparents

_____ & _____

Your Father's Siblings:

Your Father's Name

Your Name (*Maiden Name:* _____)

Your Children:

Your Grandchildren:

Your Great Grandchildren:

Maternal Great Grandparents

_____ & _____

_____ & _____

Maternal Grandparents

_____ & _____

Your Mother's Name

Your Mother's Siblings:

Congratulations

on taking the necessary steps to

PLAN YOUR OWN FUNERAL

to help assist your family & friends

with following your final wishes.

Also, thanks for all the kind words, advice, pictures,

family memories, family secrets and more

that you decided to share with your loved ones.

This book will become a keepsake for them.

Made in the USA
Middletown, DE
31 March 2023

27357716R00088